GMKH

learn

Beyond Budgeting

Building a Self-Running Financial System with Automation

INTRODUCTION

Tired of feeling chained to your budget spreadsheet? Imagine a world where your finances practically manage themselves, freeing you up to focus on what truly matters. Welcome to the power of Financial Autopilot! This book dives into a revolutionary approach called Beyond Budgeting. We'll show you how to ditch the rigid budgeting system and build a dynamic, automated financial system that works for you, 24/7.

CONTENTS

INTRODUCTION

Tired of feeling chained to your budget spreadsheet? Imagine a world where your finances practically manage themselves, freeing you up to focus on what truly matters. Welcome to the power of Financial Autopilot! This book dives into a revolutionary approach called Beyond Budgeting. We'll show you how to ditch the rigid budgeting system and build a dynamic, automated financial system that works for you, 24/7.

CHAPTER 1: THE BUDGET BLAHS: TRAPPED IN SPREADSHEETS, STRESSED BY NUMBERS?

BUDGET BLAHS!

Do you ever feel like your budget is more of a burden than a helpful tool? You spend hours meticulously crafting a spreadsheet, only to have reality throw a wrench in your perfectly planned categories. Sound familiar?

*Welcome to the club of the **Budget Blahs!** Millions of people struggle with the traditional budgeting approach. It's a cycle of frustration:*

- *Spreadsheets that Drain Your Soul: Endless rows and columns can feel overwhelming, and keeping up with data entry is a constant chore.*
- *Unrealistic Goals that Set You Up to Fail: We all get ambitious, but rigid budgets often don't account for unexpected expenses or life's curveballs.*
- *Constant Stress About Numbers: The pressure to stick to a budget can be suffocating, leading to anxiety and guilt around spending.*

But here's the good news: There's a better way! You don't have to be a slave to your spreadsheet or feel chained to unrealistic goals. Imagine a world where your finances practically manage themselves, freeing you up to focus on what truly matters.

This book will introduce you to the revolutionary concept of Financial Autopilot. We'll show you how to ditch the rigid budgeting system and build a dynamic, automated financial system that works for you, 24/7. Welcome to the club of the **Budget Blahs!** Millions of people struggle with the traditional budgeting approach. It's a cycle of frustration:

Before we blast off on this exciting journey, let's dive deeper into the common struggles with traditional budgeting:

- The Spreadsheet Blues: Remember the last time you balanced your checkbook? Yeah, spreadsheets are time-consuming and can be a major source of stress.
- The Battle of the Categories: Ever feel like your categories are too broad or too specific, making it hard to track your spending accurately?
- The Willpower Wipeout: Let's be honest, sticking to a budget perfectly is nearly impossible. Life happens, and unexpected expenses can derail your best intentions.

These are just a few of the reasons why traditional budgeting often leaves people feeling defeated. But there's hope! Financial Autopilot offers a fresh approach that eliminates these frustrations and empowers you to take control of your financial future.

This book will introduce you to the revolutionary concept of Financial Autopilot. We'll show you how to ditch the rigid budgeting system and build a dynamic, automated financial system that works for you, 24/7. Welcome to the club of the **Budget Blahs!** Millions of people struggle with the traditional budgeting approach. It's a cycle of frustration:

Before we blast off on this exciting journey, let's dive deeper into the common struggles with traditional budgeting:

- The Spreadsheet Blues: Remember the last time you balanced your checkbook? Yeah, spreadsheets are time-consuming and can be a major source of stress.
- The Battle of the Categories: Ever feel like your categories are too broad or too specific, making it hard to track your spending accurately?
- The Willpower Wipeout: Let's be honest, sticking to a budget perfectly is nearly impossible. Life happens, and unexpected expenses can derail your best intentions.

These are just a few of the reasons why traditional budgeting often leaves people feeling defeated. But there's hope! Financial Autopilot offers a fresh approach that eliminates these frustrations and empowers you to take control of your financial future.

CHAPTER 2: BEYOND THE BUDGET: FREEDOM, FLEXIBILITY, AND FINANCIAL FULFILLMENT

Imagine a world where your finances become a dance partner, not a ball and chain. Beyond Budgeting offers a dynamic approach that moves beyond the rigid structure of traditional budgeting, allowing you to waltz with your finances towards your goals.

Traditional Budgeting: A Confining Cage
Think back to the last time you wrestled with a traditional budget. Remember the frustration of:

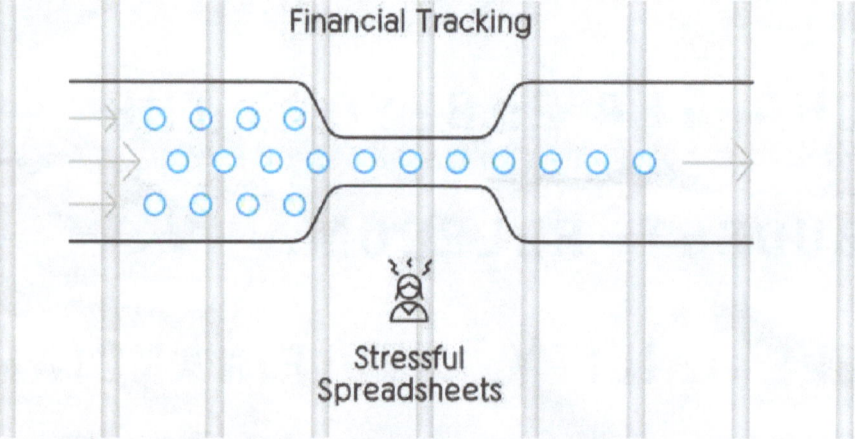

Financial Tracking

Stressful
Spreadsheets

- *Micromanaging Every Dime: Feeling trapped in a web of categories, constantly tracking every penny spent. Does this bring you closer to your dreams, or create a sense of financial claustrophobia?*
- *Unrealistic Expectations: Setting rigid goals that don't account for life's surprises. A car repair or unexpected medical bill can derail your meticulously planned budget, leaving you feeling defeated.*
- *Stressful Spreadsheets: Hours spent entering data and battling with formulas. Is this the best use of your time, or could you be focusing on strategies to grow your wealth?*

BEYOND BUDGETING: A BREATH OF FRESH AIR

Beyond Budgeting breaks free from these limitations. It's a system built on:

- **Focusing on the Big Picture:** *Drivers, Not Every Dollar. Instead of tracking every penny, Beyond Budgeting identifies the key financial drivers that truly impact your financial well-being. Think of these drivers as the engines propelling you towards your goals. Here are some examples of financial drivers:*

  - **Savings Rate:** *The percentage of your income that you consistently allocate towards your financial goals each month.*
  - *A good starting point for your savings rate is 15-20% of your income, but you can adjust this based on your individual circumstances and financial goals. For instance, if you're passionate about traveling and want to embark on a dream vacation to Europe in the next few years, you might target a higher savings rate of 30% of your income to achieve this goal faster.*
  - *Conversely, if you're nearing retirement and have already saved for a comfortable retirement lifestyle, you may aim for a lower savings rate of 10-15% of your income. Increasing your savings rate is a powerful way to grow your wealth and achieve your financial dreams, whether it's a dream vacation, a down payment on a house, or a comfortable retirement.*

- **Debt Repayment Progress:** *Debt Repayment Progress: Are you aggressively paying down debt, or are you simply making minimum payments? The faster you eliminate debt, the more financial freedom you'll have. Here's why:*

  - *Debt can be a major drain on your financial resources. Interest payments on outstanding debt eat away at your hard-earned income, limiting the amount of money you can save and invest towards your financial goals.*

  - *By prioritizing debt repayment, you free up more money each month to channel towards your savings and investments. This accelerates your financial progress and allows you to achieve your financial dreams faster.*

  - *There are different strategies for debt repayment, and the best approach for you will depend on your specific circumstances, such as the interest rates on your debts and the total amount of debt you owe. Some common debt repayment strategies include:*

- *Snowball method: This method focuses on paying off your smallest debts first, regardless of the interest rate. This can provide a sense of accomplishment and motivation as you see debts disappear from your list.*

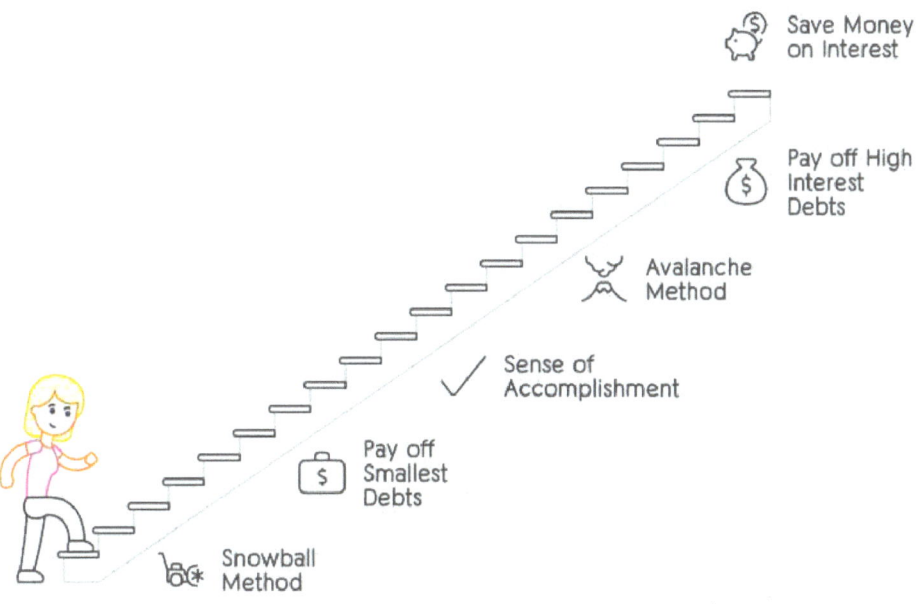

- *Avalanche method: This method prioritizes paying off the debts with the highest interest rates first. This can save you money on interest in the long run.*

- **Income Growth:** While you may not have complete control over your income, there are strategies you can explore to increase your earning potential. Here are a few ideas:

  - Negotiate a Raise: If you've been consistently exceeding expectations at your current job, consider having a conversation with your manager about a raise. Do your research beforehand to understand the average salary range for your position and experience level in your geographic location. This will help you determine a fair and competitive salary to negotiate for.
  - Skill Development: Invest in yourself by acquiring new skills or certifications that can increase your value in the workplace. This could involve taking online courses, attending workshops, or pursuing a professional development program. By expanding your skillset, you become a more attractive candidate for promotions or higher-paying job opportunities.

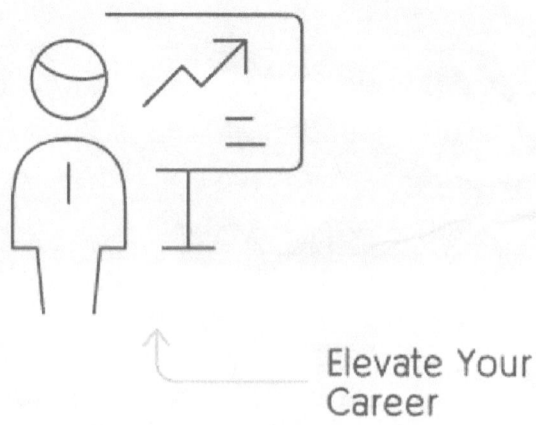

Elevate Your Career

- *Side Hustles: The gig economy offers a variety of opportunities to generate additional income outside of your traditional job. Consider your skills and interests to identify a side hustle that aligns with your strengths and passions.*

Skill Development — Side Hustles — Consider your skills and interests

Invest in yourself — The gig economy offers a variety of opportunities — Identify a side hustle that aligns with your strengths and passions

- *This could involve freelancing, starting an online business, or renting out a spare room in your home. While side hustles require some time and effort, they can be a great way to boost your income and accelerate your financial progress.*

Freelancing — Side Hustles — Online Business — Renting Out Spare Room

- *Flexibility: Your Financial GPS, Not a Rigid Map:* Beyond Budgeting recognizes that life is unpredictable. Unexpected expenses or changes in your circumstances shouldn't derail your financial journey. This system allows your financial plan to adapt, so you can adjust your goals and strategies as needed. It's like having a financial GPS system that helps you navigate unexpected detours and keeps you on track towards achieving your financial destination.

- *Automation Takes the Wheel:* Gone are the days of manually tracking every penny in a spreadsheet. Beyond Budgeting leverages technology to automate repetitive tasks like data entry and calculations. Here are a few examples of how you can leverage technology for financial automation:

- *Personal Finance Management Apps:* A variety of personal finance management apps can connect to your bank accounts and credit cards, automatically categorize your transactions, and generate spending reports. Here are a few suggestions to get you started: Mint, YNAB (You Need a Budget), and Personal Capital are just a few examples of popular personal finance management apps.

- *There are many other options available, so explore and find the app that best suits your needs and preferences. Remember, the best financial management system is the one that you'll actually use. Don't be afraid to experiment with different apps until you find one that clicks with you. Trying out a few different options is a worthwhile investment of your time, as it can lead to a system that helps you achieve your financial goals more effectively*

- *These apps can be a powerful tool for Beyond Budgeting because they allow you to:*

  - ***Track your spending:** These apps connect to your bank accounts and credit cards, automatically categorize your transactions, and generate spending reports. This saves you time and ensures your spending data is accurate and up-to-date. By tracking your spending habits, you gain valuable insights into where your money is going. This awareness is essential for identifying areas where you can cut back and free up more money to allocate towards your financial goals.*

  - ***Set budgets and goals:** Many personal finance management apps allow you to set budgets for different spending categories, such as groceries, dining out, and entertainment. You can also set savings goals for your short-term and long-term financial objectives. These apps can help you monitor your progress towards your goals and identify areas where you may need to adjust your spending habits or budgeting categories.*

  - ***Automate tasks:** Some personal finance management apps allow you to automate tasks such as bill pay reminders and category assignment for recurring transactions. This can save you time and ensure your bills are paid on time. Additionally, automatic transaction categorization eliminates the need for manual data entry, reducing the risk of errors and inconsistencies in your financial data.*

- **Bill Pay Services:** *Many banks and financial institutions offer bill pay services that allow you to schedule automatic payments for your bills. This ensures your bills are paid on time and helps you avoid late fees.*

- **Automated Transfers:** *Set up automated transfers to move money from your checking account to your savings account or investment accounts. This is a great way to automate your savings plan and ensure you're consistently saving towards your financial goals.*

- *This frees up your valuable time and mental energy to focus on big-picture financial planning and making strategic decisions to grow your wealth. Imagine the time you could save by automating tasks like bill payments, categorizing transactions, or generating financial reports. This allows you to spend more time on the things you enjoy and less time on financial drudgery.*

Beyond Budgeting is more than a system, it's a **mindset.** *It's about shifting your perspective from feeling restricted by your finances to feeling empowered to take control.*

Beyond Budgeting sets you free to dance with your money, orchestrating your financial resources to achieve your dreams and build a life filled with financial freedom and peace of mind.

CHAPTER 3: YOUR MONEY MAP: DEFINING YOUR FINANCIAL GOALS AND BUILDING A PERSONALIZED PLAN FOR SUCCESS

Congratulations! You've decided to ditch the budget blues and embrace the freedom of Beyond Budgeting. Before we set your financial autopilot on cruise control, let's take a crucial first step: charting your financial course.

Think of this chapter as creating your personalized Money Map. This map will outline your financial goals, identify your current financial position, and guide you in building a customized plan for long-term success.

Step 1: Dream Big - Defining Your Financial Goals

What does financial freedom look like for you? Is it retiring early and traveling the world? Owning your dream home? Achieving financial independence and pursuing your passions? Take some time to envision your ideal financial future.

Here are some prompts to spark your brainstorming:
- **Short-term Goals (1-3 years)**: What financial milestones do you want to achieve in the next few years? This could be saving for a down payment on a house, paying off a specific debt, or funding a dream vacation.
- **Mid-term Goals (3-5 years)**: What would you like to accomplish financially in the mid-term? This could be saving for a child's education, starting a business, or achieving a specific savings target.
- **Long-term Goals (5+ years)**: Envision your ideal financial future in the long run. Do you plan to retire early? Do you want to create a legacy for your family? Define your long-term aspirations to guide your financial decisions today.

Step 2: Know Your Numbers - Assessing Your Current Financial Situation

Now let's take a realistic snapshot of your current financial standing. Gather your financial statements, including bank account balances, credit card statements, and investment reports.

Here's what you need to focus on:

- Income: Calculate your net monthly income after taxes. This will be the foundation for building your financial plan.

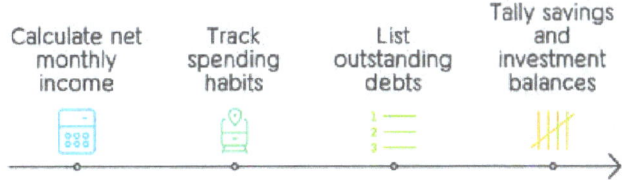

| Calculate net monthly income | Track spending habits | List outstanding debts | Tally savings and investment balances |

- Expenses: Track your spending habits for a month. Categorize your expenses to understand where your money goes. Personal finance management apps, as discussed in Chapter 2, can be helpful for tracking and analyzing your spending patterns.

- Debt: List all your outstanding debts, including credit card balances, student loans, and any other loans. Note the interest rates and minimum payments for each debt.

- Savings and Investments: Tally your current savings and investment balances. This includes your emergency fund, retirement savings accounts, and any investment accounts you may have.

Step 3: Bridging the Gap - Building Your Personalized Financial Plan

Now that you've envisioned your dream financial future (Step 1) and taken stock of your current financial situation (Step 2), it's time to build the bridge that connects them: your personalized financial plan.

Beyond Budgeting ditches the idea of rigid, static budgets, but it emphasizes smart and strategic planning.

Here's how to craft your personalized roadmap to financial freedom:

Prioritize and Sequence Your Goals: Not all goals are created equal. Imagine you want to buy a house in two years and travel to Europe in five years. Buying a house is likely a more urgent goal because it requires a larger sum of money in a shorter timeframe. So, prioritize buying a house and sequence your travel plans for later.

Identify Your Key Drivers: *Focus on the engines that move you forward.*

These drivers are the 2-3 financial factors that most significantly impact your progress towards your goals. Here are some examples:

- **Savings Rate:** *This is the percentage of your income you consistently set aside towards your financial goals each month.*
  - *Let's say your goal is to save for a down payment on a house in two years. You estimate you'll need $40,000 for a 20% down payment.*
  - *Knowing your current income, you can calculate the savings rate you need to achieve this goal within your timeframe. For instance, if your monthly income is $5,000, you'll need to save $1,667 per month to reach your $40,000 goal in two years ($40,000 / 24 months = $1,667).*
  - *This calculation helps you determine if your current savings rate is sufficient or if you need to explore strategies to increase it.*

Savings for Down Payment

Develop Actionable Strategies: *Turn plans into action! Based on your key drivers, brainstorm specific steps to move the needle. Here's an example:*

- *Goal: Increase Savings Rate for House Down Payment*
- *Key Driver: Savings Rate*
- *Actionable Strategies:*
    - *Reduce eating out by 2 times a week: Saves $50 per week*
    - *Cancel unused gym membership (if you're not using it): Saves $20 per month*
    - *Explore ways to increase income (side hustle, negotiate raise)*

Embrace Flexibility and Make Adjustments: Life throws curveballs.

Build wiggle room into your plan by creating buffers. Unexpected events happen, so be prepared to adjust your strategies or sequence your goals if needed. The beauty of Beyond Budgeting is its adaptability. Review your plan regularly, at least quarterly, and make tweaks as your circumstances or goals evolve.

Here are some examples of how you might build in flexibility:

- *Include a buffer in your monthly budget: Allocate a small amount of money each month for unexpected expenses. This can help you avoid derailing your plan if your car needs repairs or your appliance breaks down.*
- *Plan for multiple scenarios: Consider different situations that could impact your finances, such as a job loss or a medical emergency. Having a plan B in place can provide peace of mind and help you adapt your financial strategy if needed.*

- **Be willing to adjust your goals:** *Your goals and priorities may change over time. Beyond Budgeting allows you to revisit your goals and sequence them strategically based on your evolving circumstances.*

Remember, your Money Map is a living document, and the examples provided are just a starting point. Think of it as a roadmap that guides you, but one you can adjust as your financial journey unfolds. Fill in the specifics based on your unique situation and financial scenarios. Here are some prompts to get you started:

- *What are your short-term, mid-term, and long-term financial goals? Be specific and quantify your goals whenever possible (e.g., save $10,000 for a down payment in two years).*
- *What is your current income?*
- *What are your monthly expenses? Once you track your spending for a month, categorize your expenses to identify areas where you can cut back if needed.*
- *What is your current debt situation? List all your debts, including interest rates and minimum payments.*
- *What is your current savings and investment situation? Consider your emergency fund, retirement savings, and any investment accounts you may have.*

By reflecting on these questions and personalizing the examples provided in this chapter, you can build a solid foundation for your Financial Autopilot system.

In the next chapter, we'll learn about the heart of Beyond Budgeting - ditching static budgets and using rolling forecasts and driver-based planning to stay on the path to financial freedom!

CHAPTER 4: DITCH THE CRYSTAL BALL: EMBRACE ROLLING FORECASTS AND DRIVER-BASED PLANNING

Remember the frustration of meticulously crafting a budget, only to have reality throw a wrench in your perfectly planned categories? Traditional budgeting often relies on static forecasts, attempting to predict your finances months or even years into the future.

Beyond Budgeting offers a refreshing alternative: rolling forecasts and driver-based planning.

Rolling Forecasts: Adapting to the Ever-Changing Landscape

Imagine a weather forecast that only predicts the next few hours. This is the essence of a rolling forecast. Instead of a rigid, long-term prediction, Beyond Budgeting utilizes rolling forecasts that update regularly, typically every month or quarter. This allows you to:

- **Incorporate New Information and Maintain Flexibility:** Unexpected expenses, job changes, or market fluctuations can all impact your finances. Rolling forecasts prevent your financial plan from becoming outdated and irrelevant.
  - By incorporating the latest information into your plan on a regular basis, you can ensure your roadmap reflects your current financial reality.
  - This adaptability empowers you to adjust your strategies and make informed decisions as circumstances evolve. For instance, imagine you lose your job and need to dip into your emergency savings.
  - A traditional, static budget wouldn't account for this unexpected event. However, with rolling forecasts, you can adjust your plan accordingly. You might reduce your savings goals for the next few months to compensate for the funds used from your emergency savings.
  - This ensures your plan remains realistic and achievable throughout your financial journey.

Driver-Based Planning: *Focus on What Matters Most Traditional budgeting often gets bogged down in tracking every penny across numerous categories. Beyond Budgeting takes a different approach, focusing on the key financial drivers that truly impact your financial well-being.*

Here's how driver-based planning works:
- ***Identify Your Key Drivers:*** *These are the 2-3 financial factors that have the most significant influence on achieving your goals. We discussed examples in Chapter 3, such as savings rate, debt repayment progress, or income growth.*
- ***Monitor Your Drivers:*** *Track your progress on these key drivers regularly. Many personal finance management apps, as discussed previously, can automate this process and provide insightful reports on your key drivers.*
- ***Adjust Strategies Based on Your Drivers:*** *If your savings rate is lagging behind your target, explore ways to increase it (reduce expenses, find a side hustle). If your debt repayment progress is slow, consider strategies to accelerate it (debt consolidation, negotiating lower interest rates).*

Let's illustrate this with an example:
- *Goal: Save $10,000 for a down payment on a house in two years.*
- *Key Driver: Savings Rate*
- *Initial Strategy: Increase monthly savings by reducing eating out by 2 times per week.*
- *Monthly Review: After a month, you track your spending and discover you're only saving $30 per week by eating out less. This translates to $120 per month, which is short of your target increase of $167 per month needed to reach your savings goal in two years.*

Adapting Your Strategy with Driver-Based Planning:
Based on this information, you can adjust your strategy to reach your savings goal.

Here are a few options:
- **Further reduce eating out:** Explore additional ways to cut back on dining expenses, perhaps by brown-bagging lunch or utilizing meal prepping strategies.
- **Explore Additional Income Streams:** Consider taking on a side hustle or identifying other ways to increase your monthly income.
- **Negotiate a Raise:** If you've been consistently exceeding expectations at work, consider having a conversation with your manager about a raise.

By monitoring your key drivers and adapting your strategies as needed, you ensure your financial plan remains dynamic and responsive, propelling you towards your goals.

Rolling forecasts and driver-based planning are the cornerstones of Beyond Budgeting. They empower you to ditch the static, crystal ball approach of traditional budgeting and embrace a system that adapts to your ever-changing financial landscape.

CHAPTER 5: FOCUS ON WHAT MATTERS: AUTOMATE YOUR WAY TO FINANCIAL FREEDOM

Imagine a world where your finances practically manage themselves, freeing you up to focus on what truly matters in life. This is the power of Financial Autopilot in Beyond Budgeting.

We've discussed ditching static budgets and focusing on key financial drivers. Now, let's explore how technology can automate repetitive tasks and empower you to take control of your financial well-being.

Exploring Personal Finance Management Apps

The world of financial technology offers a vast array of apps and software specifically designed to automate your finances. Here's what to look for when selecting your crew:

- **Budgeting Tools:** While Beyond Budgeting focuses on driver-based planning, some apps can still be helpful for monitoring your spending habits and identifying areas for improvement. Here are some examples with features to consider:
    - **Mint:** Categorizes transactions automatically, allows you to set budgets for different spending categories, and offers insights into your spending trends.
    - **YNAB (You Need a Budget)**: Uses a unique envelope-based budgeting system to help you allocate funds towards specific goals. Provides features for monitoring spending progress within each budget category.
    - **Personal Capital:** Offers a comprehensive budgeting tool with features like transaction categorization, bill tracking, and net worth tracking. Provides customizable budgeting categories and allows you to set goals for different areas of your spending.

- **Simple**: Offers a straightforward budgeting interface with a focus on ease of use. Great for beginners or those who prefer a no-frills approach.
- **PocketGuard**: Analyzes your spending to identify areas where you can cut back and save money. Provides features like bill tracking and subscription management.
- **Goodbudget**: Uses a virtual envelope system similar to YNAB, allowing you to allocate funds towards different spending goals.

- **Goal Setting**: Look for apps that allow you to set and track both short-term and long-term financial aspirations. Visualizing your progress is a powerful motivator.
  - Turn your financial dreams into tangible goals by incorporating specific details and deadlines.
  - For instance, instead of a vague goal of "saving more money," set a **SMART** goal like "saving $5,000 for a down payment on a car within 12 months." **SMART stands for Specific, Measurable, Achievable, Relevant, and Time-bound.** By setting clear and defined goals, you'll be much more likely to achieve them.
  - The ability to track your progress towards these goals within your financial app keeps you motivated and engaged on your financial journey.

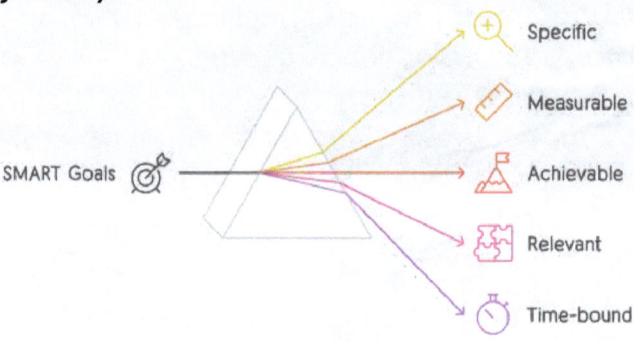

- **_Milestone Tracking and Progress Notifications:_** _Many apps offer features that can significantly boost your motivation by allowing you to set milestones and receive progress notifications. Here are a few examples:_
  - _**Mint**: Allows you to set custom progress indicators for your savings goals and receive notifications when you reach milestones._
  - _**YNAB:** Enables you to set mini-goals (milestones) for each of your budget categories. As you contribute funds towards your goals, YNAB provides motivational messages and tracks your progress visually._
  - _**You Perlu:** This app focuses specifically on goal achievement and uses a unique approach to break down large goals into smaller, manageable steps. You Perlu allows you to set milestones, track your progress visually using progress bars, and receive motivational notifications to keep you on track._

- **_Financial Tracking_**_: Connect your bank accounts and credit cards to your chosen app for automatic transaction downloads and insightful spending reports. These reports are essential for understanding your financial landscape. Here are some popular apps with robust financial tracking features:_
  - _**Mint**: Categorizes transactions automatically and provides insightful reports on your spending habits, budgeting progress, and net worth._
  - _**Personal Capital**: Offers detailed transaction categorization and spending breakdowns across various categories. Provides net worth tracking and portfolio monitoring features._
  - _**YNAB**: Categorizes transactions automatically and assigns them to your designated budget categories. Offers customizable reports to track progress towards specific goals._

Remember, the best financial management app is the one that you'll actually use. Explore different options and find one that aligns with your needs and preferences. Don't be afraid to experiment; a little time upfront can lead to a system that significantly boosts your financial progress.

Financial Automation Beyond Apps

While personal finance management apps offer valuable tools, automation extends beyond them. Here are some additional strategies:

- *Automatic Investment Plans: Many investment platforms allow you to set up automatic investment plans, contributing a specific amount of money to your investment accounts at regular intervals. This is a fantastic approach for long-term investing, such as retirement savings. By automating your investments, you ensure consistent contributions and benefit from the power of compounding over time.*
- *Salary Deductions: Consider having a portion of your paycheck automatically deposited into your savings account. This "pay yourself first" approach ensures you prioritize saving towards your financial goals.*

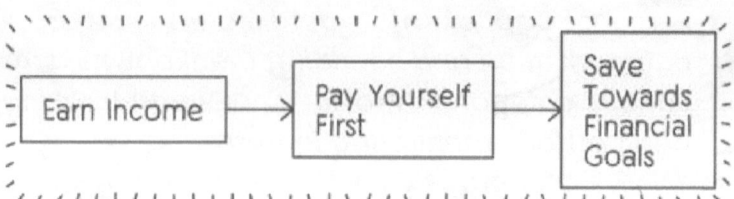

Setting Your System on Cruise Control: Effortless Automation Management

Once you've assembled your crew of financial apps and tools, it's time to set your system on autopilot. Here's how to ensure smooth sailing:

- **Seamless Implementation:** Carefully follow the instructions for each app or software you integrate. Most platforms offer user-friendly interfaces and step-by-step guides for setup.
- **Regular Monitoring:** Schedule periodic reviews to monitor your automated systems. Ensure transactions are categorized correctly, and adjust any settings as needed.
- **Adapting to Change:** Life throws curveballs. If your financial situation or goals evolve, be prepared to adapt your automated systems accordingly. The beauty of Beyond Budgeting is its flexibility.

The Benefits of Automation

By automating repetitive tasks, Financial Autopilot offers a variety of benefits:

- **Save Time:** Imagine the extra time you'll have for the things you enjoy by automating tasks like bill payments and transaction categorization. This allows you to focus on strategic financial planning and making informed investment decisions.
- **Reduce Errors:** Manual data entry can be prone to mistakes. Automation minimizes errors in your financial data, ensuring your reports and insights are accurate and reliable.
- **Stay on Track:** Automating tasks like savings transfers and bill payments helps you stay on track with your financial plan.
- **Peace of Mind:** Knowing your bills are paid on time and your savings goals are consistently funded reduces financial stress and allows you to focus on other aspects of your life.

By leveraging automation, you'll experience the freedom of a streamlined financial system. Imagine the possibilities: more time for your passions, reduced stress about finances, and the peace of mind that comes with knowing your financial ship is charting a course towards your dreams.

Set sail with confidence, engage your Financial Autopilot, and navigate your financial journey with ease!

CONCLUSION

Congratulations! You've Mastered Beyond Budgeting: A Compass for Your Financial Voyage

Welcome aboard, financially savvy sailors! We've reached the conclusion of this guide, equipping you with the tools and strategies of Beyond Budgeting to navigate your financial journey with confidence.

Let's recap the key takeaways from each chapter and set you on course for achieving your financial goals.

Chapter 1: Ditching the Budget Blahs: Embracing Beyond Budgeting

- We ditched the rigid, static budgets and embraced a dynamic system built on flexibility and adaptability. Example: Imagine a family with a fixed monthly budget for groceries. An unexpected medical expense might force them to cut back on groceries, derailing their entire budget. Beyond Budgeting allows for adjustments based on unforeseen circumstances, perhaps by utilizing emergency savings or exploring temporary cost-cutting measures like meal prepping.

Chapter 2: Charting Your Course: Goal Setting for Financial Freedom

- We emphasized the importance of clearly defining your short-term, mid-term, and long-term financial aspirations. Example: A short-term goal might be saving for a summer vacation, a mid-term goal could be saving for a down payment on a car in two years, and a long-term goal might be saving for retirement. Knowing your "why" will fuel your motivation and keep you focused throughout your financial journey.

Chapter 3: Beyond Budgeting's Guiding Principles: Flexibility and Focus

- We explored the core principles of Beyond Budgeting: rolling forecasts, driver-based planning, and breaking free from static budgets. Example: Rolling forecasts allow for updates to your financial plan based on new information. Say you receive a raise at work. You can adjust your rolling forecast to reflect increased income and potentially accelerate your savings goals. Driver-based planning focuses on the 2-3 financial factors that most significantly impact your goals. For instance, the key driver for your short-term goal of saving for a vacation might be your monthly savings rate. Increasing your savings rate through strategies like reducing eating out or taking on a side hustle will accelerate your progress towards this goal.

Chapter 4: Rolling with the Punches: Embrace Rolling Forecasts and Driver-Based Planning

- We discussed the benefits of rolling forecasts (adapting to changing circumstances) and driver-based planning (focusing on key financial drivers). Example: Imagine a couple planning their wedding. Unexpectedly, their venue costs increase. With rolling forecasts, they can adjust their financial plan to account for this additional expense. They might explore driver-based planning strategies like reducing their discretionary spending on entertainment or negotiating with vendors to find cost-saving alternatives.

Chapter 5: Autopilot Engagement: Financial Freedom Through Automation

- We explored the transformative power of automation in Beyond Budgeting, leveraging technology to streamline tasks and free up your time. Example: Automating bill payments ensures you never miss a due date and avoids late fees. Automating savings transfers removes the temptation to spend that money and keeps you on track with your financial goals. Many user-friendly apps can be your crew on this financial journey, offering features like budgeting tools, goal setting, financial tracking, and bill management. Examples of popular apps include Mint, YNAB, Personal Capital, Simple, PocketGuard, and You Perlu

In Summary:

- **Beyond Budgeting is a mindset shift**: It empowers you to take control of your finances, navigate through life's uncertainties, and build a future filled with financial security and freedom.
- **Focus on your goals**: Clearly define your financial aspirations.
- **Ditch static budgets:** Embrace rolling forecasts for flexibility.
- **Identify your key drivers:** Focus on the 2-3 financial factors that most significantly impact your goals (e.g., savings rate, debt repayment progress, income growth).
- **Embrace automation**: Leverage technology to streamline tasks and reduce errors.
- **Review and revise regularly:** Your financial plan is a living document. Adapt your strategies as needed.

To-Do List:

- **Define your financial goals.** (What do you want to achieve in the short term, mid-term, and long term?)
- **Identify your key financial drivers.** (The 2-3 factors that most impact your goals)
- **Explore personal finance management apps**. Find one that aligns with your needs and preferences.
- **Set up automated features**. (Bill payments, savings transfers, transaction categorization)
- **Schedule regular reviews.** (Monitor progress and adjust your plan as needed)

Remember, financial freedom is a journey, not a destination. Embrace the process, celebrate your milestones, and don't be discouraged by setbacks. With dedication and Beyond Budgeting as your guide, you can navigate your financial journey with confidence and build a secure and prosperous future.

See you in the next lesson!

GMKH

THANK YOU

GMKH

www.ingramcontent.com/pod-product-compliance
Lightning Source LLC
Chambersburg PA
CBHW050756290526
45792CB00008B/2203